SCOTTISH HOME COOKING

SCOTTISH HOME COOKING

To dear Sue

good friends, good food
good wine —
ahhh !
love
judy

Aug 28th 2011

JUDY PATERSON

SCOTTISH
HOME COOKING

First published 1995

by Lindsay Publications, Glasgow

© Judy Paterson

ISBN 1-898169-03-9

Front cover photograph supplied by **The Telegraph Colour Library**

Text and cover illustrations by **Gilbert Gordon**

Text layout and cover designed by **Smith & Paul Design Associates, Paisley**

Printed and bound by **Bell and Bain Ltd., Glasgow**

$\mathcal{A}$CKNOWLEDGEMENTS

Once again, many thanks to those who offered
support and encouragement and sometimes favourite recipes.
Thanks to my mother for Wysiwyg and to my family and friends
who ate their way through large portions of this book!
I especially wish to thank John, my butcher,
for advice and criticism and his wonderful
service over the years.

To the memory of my mother,
who invented Gunk!

CONTENTS

NTRODUCTION

One of my earliest memories is of a red and white tiled floor with the legs of a table in the centre, some chairs and an old-fashioned cooker with feet like a lion's paws. At the other end of the room, towering above me, was a green dresser with plates and cups hanging from hooks. It is a baby's view of the kitchen of the thatched cottage in which I lived until I was two.

When I was older, I was allowed to visit my grandfather for breakfast on Saturday mornings. He kept a special egg cup for me and I still have it. These are my earliest "kitchen" memories. Others revolve around the years of growing up with hungry brothers and the cry, "Look at the grouse!" - a ruse to catch mother's attention while the kitchen raiders made off with a handful of newly cooked chips.

Later, when I lived in Pappa New Guinea, I learned to feed a family and hold down a full-time job. There were few convenience foods. I went to the native markets and tried many of the leafy foods and I still think a baked yam is better than any potato I've tasted. I became an expert in cutting a coconut in half with one blow from a bush knife. Coconut milk was the main ingredient for the household cooking pot, excellent for softening the tough leafy greens and a wonderful base for cooking chicken!

None of these experiences equipped me for my next venture: running a small hotel in Sutherland. As with most things in life, I found that simplicity was the answer: good honest home cooking was what my guests looked for and the recipes in this collection are the result.

The emphasis is on   cooking and the presentation of simple Scottish meals. The book has been written also for those who visit Scotland and who may regard it as a souvenir of their visit. I hope it provides an insight to that most important aspect of true hospitality: good food.

During the short tourist season in the Highlands, too many casual visitors wanted "fast food". My chief delight came when my regular guests would arrive asking, "What's in the pot?"

I am an incurable romantic: picture the ancient hall of an austere baronial tower, mist from the hills swirling through the door on the plaids of the hungry clansmen. "What's in the pot?"

It would have been broth, with barley and vegetables and maybe the last of the beef.

There's an old tradition that in the Border Reiving days when only the hough or shank was left to cook, the lady of the house would serve her lord a pair of spurs on his trencher apologising to his men, "Hough i' the pot!" In other words, she was saying it was time for another cattle raid across the border!

"Hough in the Pot" was a great favourite with my guests. It is such a favourite with my family that my daughter asked to have it for her 21st!

Throughout the ages the Scots, wealthy and otherwise, relied upon whatever produce was at hand. The essence of Scottish cooking is simplicity. As with any people who rely upon the delicate balance of nature, the Scots made use of all that the land and sea had to offer.

Now, we really could not imagine dining on Crappit Heids (stuffed fish heads) and few would have the time or inclination to prepare haggis. We do, however, have the advantage of year round access to excellent produce and all the convenience of the modern kitchen. The recipes I include are primarily adaptations of traditional recipes; some are simple presentations of Scottish foods; some have been included because they not only taste good- they also sound good!

Soup

Imagine a great iron pot hanging over glowing coals.
It might be in a crofter's small earthen - floored house. It could
just as easily hang below the stone flu in the kitchen of the Laird's
castle. What was in the pot was probably kale: the staple
winter green upon which everyone relied.

Usually soup would make several meals. Sometimes
the meat was removed and served separately with bannocks,
or later in time, potatoes.

A simple rule to follow when adapting soup recipes;
beef and greens, lamb and root vegetables. If you can, and you have
the time , do make up stock which can be frozen. Otherwise,
make use of consommés or stock cubes. There is no real
substitute for game stock however,

The majority of traditional soups are hearty meals,
best suited to lunches or easy suppers, rather than served as a
first course,unless your guests arrive through the mist after
hiking through the heather!

1
~

REEN KALE

Kale, or kail, *(Brassica oleracea)* is a leafy winter green, rarely sold commercially. Instead, you can use "spring greens" or any green leafy cabbage variety. When the kale died off in Spring, Scots used nettles! An alternative if you like, and certainly a talking point for your dinner!

1lb (450g) washed greens
3 pints (1.75l) beef stock
Cream - optional
2oz (50g) oatmeal
Salt & pepper

Remove thick stalks or ribs from the greens and simmer in the stock until tender. Do not cover as this will destroy the colour. Liquidise the greens with some of the stock. Stir in the oatmeal and return to the pan with the rest of the stock. Bring it to the boil and add salt and pepper to taste.

Serve with a swirl of cream if liked and some thin oatcakes.

Serves 6

Broths made with oatmeal were generally known as Brose.

EEP BREE

The neep is the large yellow winter Swedish turnip. Its clean buttery taste makes it the ideal accompaniment to spicy haggis. This soup originated from the thrifty use of the stock which was poured over oatmeal to make a brose or thin porridge. The following variation has more body.

1¹/₂lb (³/₄ kg) turnips	*1 medium onion*
2oz (50g) butter	*1¹/₂ pints (750ml) chicken stock*
Salt & pepper	*Pinch of Cumin*
Cream - optional	*Green garnish, chives, parsley*

Peel and dice the turnip and blanch in boiling water. Drain and add to the butter which has melted in large saucepan. Add the roughly chopped onion and the cumin and sweat the vegetables gently for about 10 minutes. Add the hot stock, a little salt and pepper and simmer gently for about 30 to 40 minutes when the turnip should be thoroughly cooked.

Liquidise the vegetables in some of the stock, add to remaining stock and bring back to simmering point. Adjust the seasoning. Serve with cream if liked and a small amount of garnish.

Serves 6

Cumin and pepper were paid as a form of rent as early as
the thirteenth century.

HAIRST BREE

This is a Harvest broth- a soup made from all the young, fresh goodness of a summer's crop. It was only after 1745 when the Highlands were opened up that many of these vegetables became commonly available and were grown in the kale yards.

8oz (225g) neck of lamb
2 pints (1.15l) water
½ small head cauliflower
4oz (100g) shelled peas
Heart of a lettuce
Chopped parsley

3 carrots
2 white new turnips
1 bunch spring onions
4oz (100g) broad beans
1 teaspoon of sugar
Salt & pepper

Trim the fat from the lamb and bring to the boil in the water with salt. Remove any scum and boil for about ³/₄ hour. Remove the meat, dice and return to the pan with diced turnips, carrots, sliced onions and the broad beans. Add cauliflower florets and simmer for another 40 minutes. Add the peas and shredded lettuce and cook for another 10 minutes. Add the sugar and adjust the seasoning. Serve hot with a garnish of parsley.

Serves 6

Often called Hotch Potch, this soup can be made with whatever is at hand.

4
~

AWD BREE

This is a simple adaptation of a traditional hare soup. Reserve the saddle and hindquarters of the hare for stewing (*see p. 34-35*)

Forequarters and rib cage of hare.	*Instant potato flakes*
1 tablespoon redcurrant or	*Butter or oil*
rowan jelly	*1 onion*
4oz (100g) streaky bacon	*1 carrot*
2 stalks celery	*Pinch mixed herbs*
4oz (100g) turnip	*Glass of port*
Salt & pepper	*Vinegar*

Rinse the hare in cold water with a little vinegar. Brown chopped bacon and onion, add the hare and sufficient water to cover well. Add salt and freshly ground pepper and simmer for 2 hours. Add the diced vegetables and herbs and simmer for a further 2 hours. Strain the stock into a clean pan. Remove meat from the carcass, shred and return to the soup. Bring to the boil and thicken *slightly* with potato flakes. Stir in the port and the jelly and serve very hot.

An alternative is to liquidise and include the vegetables for a more hearty soup.

*P*ARTAN BREE

*P*artan is the Scottish word for crab which is plentiful in certain areas. They are generally sold cooked by the fishmonger. Fish stock cubes make a wise investment.

A large crab	*3oz (75g) rice*
1 pint (600ml) milk	*1 pint (600ml) fish stock*
Anchovy essence (optional)	*$\frac{1}{2}$ pint (300ml) cream*
Salt & pepper	*Pinch of mace*

Boil the rice in the milk until soft but not mushy. Reserve the crab meat from the claws and place the rest of the meat with the cooked rice and milk into a blender. Liquidize briefly and return to a clean pan. Add the stock, the mace and a very small amount of anchovy essence if used. Taste. Adjust the seasoning if required and add more stock if a thinner soup is liked. Reheat gently, stirring in the cream. Do not boil. Serve garnished with claw meat.

Serves 4-6

You may substitute 1lb (450g) of tinned or frozen crab meat but the soup will lack a little in flavour.

SKINK

I have to include this because of the name. It is an "Old Scots Stew Soup" and is nothing more than a cottage soup, very like Scotch Broth. This is a simple variation since few of us would consider starting with a leg of beef and a gallon of water! It is important however to use the "poorer" cuts of beef, hough or shin beef, or skirt, for their flavour. The better part of the leg of meat would have been served at a separate meal.

1lb (450g) hough (shin)	*3 pints (1.75l) water*
1lb (450g) cut vegetables	*Salt & pepper*
4oz (100g) shredded cabbage	*Mixed herbs*

Simmer the meat very gently for a minimum of four hours. Skim off any scum during cooking. Strain the stock and reserve the meat which should be shredded. Add all the vegetables except the cabbage and cook until tender. Add the herbs, seasoning to taste and finally the cabbage. Cook for 10 minutes more. Add the meat and serve very hot.   ***Serves 6***

If you have a slow cooker, the making of good rich stock is simplified. Cook the meat overnight on low and then proceed as above, adding the stock and vegetables to a saucepan and complete the cooking on the stove top.

7
~

CULLEN SKINK

The fishing traditions of the North-Eastern villages like Cullen were influenced by links with Scandinavia and a wide variety of smoked fish resulted. Finnan Haddock is the basis of this recipe but other, non-dyed smoked white fish may be substituted.

Large Finnan haddock or
8oz (250g) smoke fillet
1 onion, chopped
1lb (450g) mashed potato
Cream and parsley for garnish

2 pints (1l) water
¹/₂ pint (300ml) milk
Salt & pepper
1oz (25g) butter

Place the fish, onion and seasoning in the water and bring to the boil. Cover and simmer for 20 minutes, after which the fish will be cooked. Remove it and take the flesh from the bones. For a really good stock, return the skin and bones to the stock and simmer gently for almost an hour. Strain the stock.

Boil the milk and add it to the stock with the flaked fish and butter. Bring it back to simmering point and stir in enough mashed potato to make a creamy thick soup. Check the seasoning. Garnish with cream and parsley.   ***Serves 6***

You may like to alter the proportions of milk and water:
1¹/₂ pints (900ml) water and 1 pint (600ml) milk.

EATHER FOWLIE

Here's another soup with romantic tradition and an unusual name. It is a variation on the recipe of Lady Clark of Tillypronie, c.1880, who felt the origins lay in the Auld Alliance.

2 large chicken joints	Stock cube	Salt & pepper
1 stick celery, sliced	Cream	3 egg yolks
1 onion chopped	4oz (100g) bacon	Sprig of parsley
Pinch mace	1 carrot, sliced	Chopped parsley
3 pints (1.75l) water	Bouquet garni	

Soak the joints in salted water for $\frac{1}{2}$ hour, drain and rinse well. Place them in a large pan with the chopped bacon, stock cube, vegetables, seasoning and herbs. Bring them to the boil in the water and then simmer for an hour or more until the chicken falls from the bone. Strain the stock and remove any grease. Remove the meat from the bones and chop it finely before returning to the stock. Bring to simmering.

Beat the egg yolks with two tablespoons of cream. Add some warm stock to the egg mixture and then add it to the soup which should be off the boil. Stir thoroughly over the heat, stir in a tablespoon of chopped parsley and serve immediately. ***Serves 6.***

POACHER'S SOUP

I have adapted this recipe from that of Meg Dods's whose own inspiration was drawn from a scene in Sir Walter Scott's "Guy Mannering". This is a hearty "gypsy" soup and as with all game cooking, it relies on excellent stock.

3 pints (1.75l) game stock
1-1¹/₂lb (450-675g) game,
  grouse, venison, hare etc.
2 sticks sliced celery
Glass red wine or port
Tablespoon mushroom ketchup
4-6 eschallots

Pinch allspice
Salt & pepper
8oz (225g) potatoes
4oz (100g) cabbage
pinch cayenne

Cut the game into small dice or joints and place it with the stock and the seasonings and wine into a large pan. Bring to the boil and simmer gently for 1-2 hours until the game is tender. Remove the joint and strip the meat from the bones and return it to the pan with the potatoes to cook for a further ten minutes. Add the shredded cabbage and cook for another ten minutes. Adjust the seasoning and serve very hot.

For a thicker, smoother texture cook the vegetables with the game. Remove the meat as above and puree or blend the stock and vegetables with some of the meat. Return the rest of the meat in small pieces and bring back to the boil.

Carrot may be substituted for the cabbage. **Serves 6-8**

BARLEY BREE

This wholesome soup has a bland flavour, depending rather on its heartiness for its continuing popularity. A "country soup" it can be made with either beef or lamb or both. It is also a winter soup, otherwise known as Scotch Broth.

1lb (450g) trimmed neck lamb, or stewing beef	3 pints (1.74l) water
1oz (25g) pearl barley	Salt & pepper
2oz (50g) split peas, soaked	1 carrot diced
12oz (350g) turnip, diced	1 onion, sliced
4oz (100g) shredded cabbage	1 leek, sliced
1-2 stock cubes, optional	Tablespoon chopped parsley

Put the meat into a large saucepan with the water and bring to the boil. Skim, add seasonings, the barley and soaked peas. Simmer for 30 minutes and then add all the vegetables except the cabbage. Simmer for 1¹/₂ hours. The meat should be tender enough to roughly sliced Into pieces. Add the cabbage and adjust the seasoning and cook a further 20 minutes, stirring in the parsley just before serving.

Serves 6-8

This is a very thick soup and you may wish to add extra stock during the cooking.

COCK-a-LEEKIE

Traditionally this soup is made by first preparing a stock using a chicken with its giblets. The meat is then removed to be used for some other recipe. Cock - a- Leekie is a clear soup and as with any old Scottish recipe using chicken it is a festive dish, often appearing on Burns Night menus. The following is a simplified adaptation.

> *4 pints (2.25l) chicken stock, or water and stock cubes*
> *6 leeks cleaned and sliced*
> *Salt & pepper*
> *2 tablespoons rice*

Bring the stock to the boil and add the leeks and rice and seasoning. Simmer gently for 30 minutes. Adjust the seasoning and serve very hot.

Serves 6-8

Prunes are considered a traditional addition to the soup. If liked, add "ready to eat" stoned prunes during the last few minutes of cooking. Just one per person is sufficient.

STARTERS

The custom of serving meals in several courses
developed in the 18th century so that by 1826 Meg Dods wrote,
*"To the credit of the age, modern fashion inclines more to a few dishes, well
selected and elegantly disposed, than to that heterogeneous accumulation of
good things which notable British housewives
used to cover their table linen."*

Today our best restaurants serve imaginatively
presented dishes as "starters" to whet the appetite. The emphasis
is on taste as well as being attractive to the eye. Frequently
it is an opportunity to sample a seasonal luxury.

Preparing starters at home for
festive occasions can be easy and often they can
be prepared well in advance.

SMOKED PHEASANT WITH MUSHROOMS

Per person:

> *3 slices of smoked pheasant*
>
> *A large Vol au Vent*
>
> *1 or 2 open cap mushrooms*

Mushroom sauce:

> *Finely chopped mushrooms, moistened with heated*
> *creamy mushroom soup.*

Garnish:

> *Redcurrant or Sloe Jelly and sprigs of parsley*

Have the pheasant slices warm and either grill the mushrooms with a little butter or drizzle olive oil on them and heat them for a minute or two in the microwave.

Assemble on warm plates by placing a Vol au Vent, two mushrooms and a fan of three slices of pheasant per person. Fill the Vol au Vent with hot mushroom sauce and put a small amount of red jelly on the fan of pheasant. Add the sprig of parsley.

MOKED MACKEREL PATÉ

This will make just over 2lb (900g) of paté. For a starter, allow about 3oz (75g) per person. Making a larger quantity has advantages- there will be plenty for family use after the party.

1¹/₂ lb (725g) smoked mackerel	*Salt*
4oz (100g) fresh white	*4oz (100g) butter*
bread crumbs	*Juice of ¹/₂ lemon*
3oz (75g) cream cheese	*Fresh ground pepper*

Skin and flake the mackerel fillets and mix with the bread crumbs. Melt the butter and blend with the cream cheese and add the flaked fish mixture. Add the lemon juice and seasoning and beat until smooth.

Or, skin and flake the mackerel, melt the butter and put all the ingredients into a blender and puree. Unceremonious but quick. Serve in individual pots or line an oblong dish with cling film, chill and turn out to serve on a dish for slicing at the table. Garnish with twists of lemon.

Serve with Melba toast, water biscuits or, for a more substantial snack, oatcakes.

# HAGGIS IN NEEP NESTS

This is a really simple starter, one I use for visitors from abroad. It is an ideal way for guests to sample a dish they may otherwise be too suspicious to try. Half a small haggis will serve 4-6 people, depending on portions.

Haggis
Mashed potatoes
Turnip
Salt & pepper

Prepare the whole haggis by boiling for 1-1$^1/_2$ hours or cut the haggis in half and cook it in the microwave for a few minutes in a covered dish. With a fork break up the haggis, stir and cook a few more minutes.

Boil a suitable amount of diced turnip until tender, puree and stiffen with a little mashed potato. Keep hot until ready to serve.

Pipe or fashion nests with the neep mixture and pile 2-3oz (75g) haggis in the centre.

Decorate with a sprig of heather and serve with a nip of whisky.

SCALLOPED SHRIMPS

8oz (225g) peeled shrimps
8 tablespoons double cream
small packet potato crisps
1 egg beaten

2oz (50g) butter
Creamed potato
Salt & pepper

Butter the edges of 4 scallop shells or dishes and pipe an edging of the creamed potato on to each shell. Brush with the beaten egg and bake in a hot oven, 425°F/ 220°C/ Gas mark 7. Allow them to brown and remove from the oven, lowering the temperature to 375°F/190°C/ Gas mark 5. Divide the prawns evenly into the centre of each. Put 2 tablespoons of cream over each pile of prawns and season lightly.

Crumble the crisps finely and put just enough over each dish to cover the cream. Return to the oven and bake for 5-7 minutes to heat through.

VARIATION: *Shrimps Au Gratin* may be prepared very simply by spooning white sauce over the shrimps, covering with grated cheese and browning under a medium heat in the grill. You may need extra shrimps since the potato border is omitted.

 SHRIMP PASTE

1lb (450g) cooked shrimps
or prawns
3 anchovy fillets
Pinch of mace

1lb (450g) white fish fillets
³/₄lb (350g) butter
Pinch of cayenne

Shell the shrimps or prawns and chop them roughly. Cook the fish in a little water until it flakes easily (or cook in a covered dish in the microwave without water). Reserve 2oz (50g) of butter and melt the rest.

Put the white fish, the melted butter, the anchovy fillets and the seasonings into a blender and make into a paste. Tip into a bowl and stir the prawns in gently but thoroughly. Adjust the seasoning.

Divide the mixture into individual dishes or pots or fill larger dish. Press down firmly and place in the refrigerator until quite cold.

Melt the remaining butter and pour over the top of the paste to seal it. Return to the refrigerator until required.

Serve with melba toast or water biscuits and some salads.
Garnish with a wedge of lemon.

Serves 6 or more.

ERBRIDEAN CATCH

It is easy to forget that shellfish was part of the staple diet of Island folk many years ago. Freshly caught, it was prepared in the simplest manner. This adaptation will either make elegant canapés or an unusual starter.

Prepare croûtons by cutting shapes from slices of white bread. Fry gently on both sides in a mixture of oil and butter until they are crisp and golden. Drain on paper. They may be kept warm for immediate use or made in advance, left to cool and stored in an airtight container.

> *Shellfish*
> *Seasoned flour*
> *Crisply fried crumbled bacon*
> *Butter*

Put the shellfish into cold water and bring to the boil. Cook only until the shells open. Remove the flesh and drop into well seasoned flour. Toss and remove excess flour. Lightly fry the assorted shellfish in butter. Lay them on the warm croûtons and sprinkle with the crumbled bacon.

Allow anything from three to five per person depending on the size of the croûton and the shellfish. Garnish with a sprinkle of chopped parsley to decorate the plate and add a slice of lemon

 AYSIDE TANG

Here's a simple starter which celebrates the association of oranges with Tayside and the city of Dundee, famous for its marmalade.

2 oranges	2oz (50g) finely grated cheddar
4oz (100g) Scottish cheddar, diced	Salt & pepper
1 grapefruit	2 tablespoons milk
4 slices of orange	Salt & pepper
Dressing: 2 tablespoons mayonnaise	Paprika
3 tablespoons lemon juice	

Peel the oranges and grapefruit and remove thick membranes from the segments. Cut into bite sizes and place in a bowl with the diced cheese.

Combine the mayonnaise, grated cheese, lemon juice and seasonings. Pour it over the fruit and cheese.

Serve in individual dishes and garnish with a sprinkle of paprika and a twist of orange.

Serves 4

$\mathcal{T}$IPSY ORANGES

This is best served when oranges are large. They can be prepared well in advance of a dinner party and then finished off at the last moment.

Allow half a large orange per person
Brown sugar
Drambuie
Mint leaves

Halve the orange and run a grapefruit knife round the inside of the skin to free the flesh. Cut across the flesh into bite sized pieces. Squeeze a little of the juice out and then spoon over some Drambuie. Do not be too generous or you will lose the taste of the orange. Leave at room temperature until ready to serve.

Prepare a hot grill. Sprinkle the tops with brown sugar and grill for a few moments so that the sugar starts to bubble. Remove to individual serving dishes and decorate with a sprig of mint.

The Drambuie and orange complement each other so well it is not always easy for people to pick the "secret" of this refreshing starter.

$\mathscr{S}$MOKED SALMON

Smoked salmon is traditionally a luxurious treat and makes an ideal starter for an elegant dinner. Here are a few simple ideas.

ASPARAGUS PARCEL

Wrap three asparagus spears in a slice of smoked salmon. Garnish with parsley and a wedge of lemon and serve with brown bread and butter.

SUMMER SALMON KEBAB

Cut chunks of orange Giaia melon, green Honeydew melon, and short lengths of asparagus. Have some cherry tomatoes or even strawberries. Wrap salmon round the asparagus and thread these alternately with a selection of the fruits onto a kebab stick. Serve on a plate garnished with slices of Kiwi fruit, a fan of sliced strawberry and a wedge of lemon.

SMOKED SALMON AND SALAD

This is the way smoked salmon is usually served, allowing the salmon to be enjoyed for itself. $1^1/_2$ - 2oz (30g-50g) is sufficient per person. Arrange the salmon on the plates and place a selection of green salad leaves at the edge. Add a wedge of tomato for colour and a wedge of lemon. Serve with brown bread and butter.

FISH

Looking at a map of Scotland it is easy to see why fish was the most accessible form of protein down through the centuries. Archaeological finds in Fife show cod was on the supper menu quite frequently about 6500BC.

The country is crossed with rivers and burns and punctuated by lochs. Silvery trout wait to be tickled while salmon actually travel halfway across the world in order to make themselves available to Scottish dinner tables.

The seas offer an abundance, from the humble herring to the handsome halibut and there are many traditional methods of preparation.

In bygone days, in the islands, skate was tenderised by laying it on the grass and covering it with turf. Otherwise it was hung, unsalted, for a few days until it was "high"- an unappetising pun, as far as I can imagine. I first tasted Skate Wings in Paris and subsequently found a recipe from Elizabeth Cleland, "A New and Easy Method of Cookery", 1759. I include an adaptation of her recipe. It does not require hanging!

Today we are very conscious of conserving the riches of the seas. We can "farm" trout and oysters. For many in the past, fish was a way of life. In keeping with the tradition of simplicity, the recipes I include are quite homely offerings.

$\mathcal{T}$ROUT AND GROUSE

Here's a simple but dramatic dish to prepare for that special evening.
You should alter the name to suit the whisky you have chosen to use,

> *2 trout, cleaned*
> *1oz (25g) butter*
> *2 tablespoons Grouse Whisky*
> *Seasoned flour*
> *2oz (50g) flaked almonds*
> *1 lemon*

Brown the almond flakes under the grill. Dust the trout thoroughly with
seasoned flour. Melt the butter in a fry pan and when it bubbles lay in the fish.
Cook for 4-5 minutes on each side, adding the almonds for the last two
minutes. Stir them round to prevent them burning. Remove the pan from the
heat and pour in the whisky. Set alight and shake the pan until the flame dies.

Serve with lemon wedges, a side salad, and chips in serving dish.

Serves 2

SKATE WINGS

4 skate wings
2oz (50g) butter
4oz (100g) wholegrain mustard
Court Bouillon (fish stock)
Chopped parsley

Lay the skate wings in a dish and cover with court bouillon, cover and cook at 400°F/200°C/ or gas mark 4, for about half an hour. Test by seeing if the flesh is firm and is shrinking from the bone. Alternatively, cook on high in a microwave allowing approximately 5 minutes per pound.

Melt the butter and combine with the mustard. When the fish is cooked, use 4 tablespoons of the cooking fluid to add to the mustard mixture.

Place the fish onto warmed plates and pour the sauce over. Decorate the plate at the edge with a sprinkle of parsley and serve with creamy mashed potatoes and fresh vegetables, lightly cooked.

Serves 4

ARTAN PIE

This variation of Meg Dods's recipe makes an elegant supper. Fishmongers sell dressed crabs in season and so this is a very quick dish to prepare. Choose a good white wine so that it can also be used to accompany the meal.

2 dressed crabs
Glass dry white wine (approx.)
4 tablespoons bread crumbs
Tabasco (optional)
2oz (50g) butter

Slices of toast
Pinch nutmeg
Salt & white pepper
Extra butter, melted
Lemon wedges

In a bowl, soak 2 tablespoons of bread crumbs in half of the wine, stir in the nutmeg, a little salt and pepper and a dash of Tabasco if liked. Remove the crab meat from the shells and fork it into the wine mixture. If it is very thick add a little more wine and adjust the seasoning.

In a pan, melt the butter and sauté the mixture so that it warms through. Prepare a hot grill.

In a pan, melt the butter and sauté the mixture so that it warms through. Prepare a hot grill.

Return the crab to the shells, sprinkle thickly with bread crumbs and drizzle melted butter over the top. Put under a hot grill to brown the top and serve immediately with hot toast and lemon wedges.

A side salad of chopped tomatoes, cucumber, onions and cress, will add contrast to the richness of the crab.   *Serves 2*

ALMON

Even now that it is available year round, salmon is such a luxury that it seems a pity to spoil its natural flavours with the old fashioned sauces which often masked a not - quite- fresh fish. Choose steaks which are of even size and thickness. I prefer to cook salmon in the microwave: it is quick, clean and prevents drying out. The fish continues to "cook" for a minute or so once it is removed from the oven, allowing ample time to serve up the vegetables without the fish cooling.

4 salmon steaks, 1" ($2^1/_2$ cm) thick	*Lemon juice*
Lemon wedges	*Salt & pepper*

Have the fish at room temperature. Place the salmon so that the "tails" of the steaks are interleaved in the centre of a dish suitable for the microwave. Put some lemon juice over the centre bone of each steak to help reduce the "popping". Sprinkle with a tiny amount of salt and pepper. Cover the dish with grease proof paper. Cook a total of 4 minutes per pound (450g). You may like to turn the pieces half way through cooking, in which case, use a little more lemon juice over the central bone.

Serve with vegetables or salads and lemon wedges. **Serves 4**

You may grill in a preheated pan with butter for about 8 minutes, depending on the thickness of the steaks.

ALMOM GATEAU

Here is something slightly grander than fish cakes. It is a good way to use up leftover salmon or other fish. You may be able to buy salmon scraps, even tinned salmon would do. If you have a spring form cake tin, or one with a removable bottom, it will make the task of removing the cake easier. Alternativley, line a tin with foil and leave the edges so that you can remove it easily.

$^1/_2$ lb (225g) cooked salmon	1 egg beaten
$^3/_4$ lb (350g) mashed potato	1 teaspoon parsley
2 tablespoons white sauce	Medium oatmeal
Salt & pepper	2 drops anchovy sauce
$^1/_2$ finely chopped onion	Grated cheese

Grease the tin and coat with oatmeal. Set the oven at 350°F/ 180°C/ Gas mark 4.

Flake the fish and combine all the ingredients except the cheese. Put into the tin, cover with grease proof paper and cook for 30 to 40 minutes. Sprinkle some grated cheese over the top and brown quickly under a hot grill.

Remove the cake from the tin and serve at the table with salads or vegetables and a parsley, mustard, or cheese sauce. **Serves 4**

VIKING COD WITH MUSTARD SAUCE

This adaptation of a traditional recipe recalls Scottish links with Scandinavia.

4 cod steaks
4 sprigs parsley
4 bayleaves
1½ tablespoons flour
1 teaspoon made English mustard
1 tablespoon vinegar (optional)

½ pint (300ml) milk
½ pint (300ml) water
Pinch salt
Freshly ground pepper
2oz (50g) butter

Lay each steak over a sprig of parsley and a bayleaf in a shallow fry pan. Sprinkle with a little salt and pepper and add the milk and water, bring to the boil gently and simmer for about 10 minutes. Remove the fish to a covered dish and keep hot. Reserve the strained cooking liquid. In the pan, melt the butter over a low heat and stir in the flour, gradually adding the fish liquor to make a sauce. Increase the heat, stirring to prevent lumps and when the sauce is thickened add the mustard (and vinegar if liked). More mustard may be added for a stronger taste. Adjust the seasonings. Place the cod on warm plates and pour a little sauce over. Garnish with parsley.

Serve this with skirlie or clapshot and you have a real talking point for visitors from abroad! **Serves 4.**

FISHERMAN'S PIE

Use this as the basis for any family dinner or a robust lunch in winter time. Vary the fish according to what is available.

1-1¹/₄lb (450-575g) cooked fish,
either smoked haddock, or an
assortment of white and shelled fish
³/₄ pint (450g) white sauce
1lb (450g) mashed potato
2 onions, chopped
Seasonings
Grated cheese
Butter

Sauté the onions until soft. Flake the fish and mix with the onions and the sauce. Season and place into a dish. Cover with mashed potatoes, dot with butter and sprinkle with grated cheese.

Bake at 400°F/ 200°C/ Gas mark 7. *Serves 4*

GAME AND FOWL

Game is definitely my favourite food to cook and serve.
I enjoy its earthy open-air flavours and the rich methods of preparation.
It tells of romance and the medieval rights of kings and
the equally legendary rights of the
poacher and gypsy.

There are a number of excellent books on the subject of
game cooking and I enjoy the creations of these cooks. But I favour
the uncluttered tastes of simple presentation which I
feel reflects the roots of Scottish home cooking
through the ages.

Like other seasonal luxuries, Game can be procured
almost all year round. The use of a Slow Cooker approximates the
traditional pot- hung- over- the - fire, which was used in the
homes of rich and poor alike as the means of cooking. If you
don't own one I would heartily recommend
it as a real asset.

# GYPSY STEW

1 rabbit jointed,	*1 pint (600ml) stock*
washed and dried	*1-2 onions*
Butter or oil	*6-8 peppercorns*
3-4 cloves	*Teaspoon lemon juice*
4oz (100g) diced bacon	*Salt & pepper*
Bouquet Garni	*1¹/₂oz (35g) flour*
A glass or two of good red wine	

Fry the rabbit joints in oil or butter and sprinkle with flour. Put them in a deep casserole dish. Lightly fry the diced bacon and add to the rabbit. Stick the cloves into the onions and nestle them between the joints. Add 1 glass of wine and the other ingredients, season lightly, cover and cook on one of the following ways:

Cook for one hour 350°F/180°C/Gas mark 4 in the oven and then lower the temperature to 300°F / 180°C / Gas mark 2 and cook a further two hours.

Or

Simmer gently on the stove for 2¹/₂- 3 hours. Cook for 7-10 hours on "Low" in a slow cooker. ¹/₂ hour before the cooking is complete check the sauce and thicken with granules or a little more flour slaked with water. Add more wine if liked.   ***Serves 4.***

VARIATIONS
(Gypsy Stew)

You may like to substitute tiny pickling onions or shallots for the onions. Stick a clove into four of them and distribute them evenly round the joints.

Vegetables such as sliced or diced carrot and celery may be added and or even tiny button mushrooms.

Hare can be cooked in the same way. You might use the saddle and hindquarters after making Bawd Bree with the forequarters. If a whole hare is used you will need extra stock and extra wine.

Serve with fluffy mashed potatoes and lightly boiled fresh vegetables and a game jelly such as redcurrant or rowan. Forcemeat balls are traditional, festive and economical.

FORCEMEATBALLS

4oz (100g) fresh bread crumbs
$\frac{1}{2}$ teaspoon mixed herbs
2oz (50g) melted butter
1 rabbit or chicken liver, minced
Squeeze of lemon juice
2 teaspoons chopped parsley
1 egg beaten
$\frac{1}{2}$ onion finely chopped
1oz (25g) minced bacon
Salt & pepper
Pinch of nutmeg.

Combine the ingredients and form into balls. Deep fry and add to the stew just before serving.

INGDOM OF FIFE PIE

1-2 rabbits (1¹/₂lb, 750g meat off the carcass)
hard boiled egg (optional)
Salt & pepper
1lb (450g) pickled pork
1lb (450g) puff pastry
¹/₄ teaspoon nutmeg
¹/₂ portion of uncooked Forcemeat (see p34)

Soak the rabbit in salted water for at least an hour. Strip the meat from the bones and put aside. Using the carcass, make a stock by simmering it in fresh water for an hour or more. You will need about ¹/₂ pint (300ml).

Place the rabbit meat and pickled pork, which may be sliced or diced, into a deep pie dish along with the Forcemeat balls and the sliced hard boiled egg if used. Season each layer with salt, pepper and nutmeg. The dish should be well packed down. Pour in sufficient stock to moisten the meats. Cover with a pastry which should be glazed with a little milk and make 3 or 4 ventilation slits to allow steam to escape.

Bake at 400°F/ 200°C/ Gas mark 6 for 15 minutes and then lower the heat and bake at 325°F/ 170°C/ Gas mark 3 for a further 1¹/₄-1¹/₂ hours. ***Serves 8-10***

If the pie is to be eaten cold, allow it to cool thoroughly at room temperature before refrigerating. The stock will turn to jelly holding the meats firmly for slicing.

If you do not have time to prepare stock, use a good consommé.

Meg Dods's original recipe allows the rabbit joints to be cooked on the bone and you may prefer to try it this way. If the pie is to be served cold however, I do think it is nicer to remove the bones.

The pickling of meats was a traditional way of preserving and is not so popular these days. You will probably have to ask your butcher to pickle the pork for you, in which case, have two or three pounds done. I like to prepare two or three pies at once and freeze them: ideal for summer picnics, or to have at hand for visitors.

My butcher was quite intrigued with this recipe saying he hadn't pickled pork in a long time. Apparently pickled beef was a favourite weekend treat locally, but he hadn't heard of this pie! I took him up a slice for testing and came away with his approval.

If you cannot get pickled pork he suggests using a mildly cured bacon cut in thick pieces.

AMILY ROAST PHEASANT

1-2 oven- ready pheasants | *Stuffing (see below)*
Butter, oil or bacon fat for browning | *4-6 rashers of streaky bacon, rolled*

Stuff the pheasants and re-tie the legs so they are close to the body. Weigh them. Set the oven to 425°F/ 220°C/ Gas mark 7. In a fry pan, brown the birds thoroughly for about 10 minutes. Place them in a roasting tin on their sides. This helps prevent the breast meat drying out. Place the bacon rolls around the birds and pour over the fats in which the birds were browned. Add an extra mixture of hot oil and butter if required. Cook quickly, turning the birds frequently, from one side to the other, and baste thoroughly each time.

Cooking Times: calculate 5 minutes for each 4oz(100g) of the bird, stuffed. If one bird weighs less, put in the oven after the heavier bird. Cooking times will vary between 25 to 30 minutes on average.

After the correct cooking and basting at this high temperature, switch off the oven and leave the door open a little. Drain off all the cooking fats and allow the birds to rest for 10 to 20 minutes in the cooling oven.

A small pheasant serves two to three people when carved in thin slices and served with the stuffing, bacon rolls and other traditional accompaniments. *(see page 40)*

VENISON CASSEROLE

2¹/₂ lb (1.1kg) stewing venison

Marinade

¹/₂ bottle red wine	*2 cloves garlic, crushed*	*2oz (50g) butter*
2 sliced onions	*4oz (100g) bacon*	*¹/₄ pint (150ml) stock*
2 sliced carrots	*Glass port*	*Rowan jelly*
8 juniper berries	*Seasoned flour*	*Salt & pepper*
Bouquet garni		

 Slightly bruise the juniper berries with the back of a wooden spoon. Put the venison into a bowl with all the marinade ingredients and leave overnight.

Take out the meat and drain then dry with kitchen paper. Toss it in the seasoned flour. Dice the bacon and fry lightly in the butter. Put it in a casserole. Brown the venison and add to the casserole. Remove the bouquet garni, and pour the marinade into the frying pan and stir in the browned flour in the pan. Bring to the boil and simmer for a few minutes. Add the stock, season lightly and pour over the venison.

Cook on "Low" for 8-10 hours in a slow cooker.

¹/₂ hour before finishing, add the port and a tablespoon of Rowan jelly.

Serves 6.

GROUSE COOKED IN CASSEROLE

Adapted from Mrs Dowie's Recipe

2 grouse with hearts, livers and necks,
    if possible. If not, substitute a chicken
    liver which adds flavour to the stock.
4oz (100g) butter
Good pinch cayenne

$^1/_4$ *pint (150ml) beef or*
    game stock
White pepper and salt
$^1/_4$ *teaspoon mace*

W ork the seasonings into the butter and adjust to your liking but do not leave out the cayenne. Divide the mixture into four. Roll two portions into balls and place one inside each bird. Put the birds, hearts, livers and necks into a casserole. Add a small amount of the stock, not more than half. Spread the remaining seasoned butter over the birds, cover and cook in the oven at 325°F/ 170°C/ Gas mark 3 for 2-2$^1/_2$ hours. Baste several times with the buttery stock. Add extra stock only if essential.

Before serving remove the hearts and necks from the stock. Mash or puree the liver into the stock to make a gravy, adding extra stock if required.

Serve on thick slices of trimmed toast with traditional trimmings for game. *(see page 43)*

Serves 2

BREAD SAUCE

1 medium onion	*Salt and white pepper*
³/₄ pint (450ml) milk	*4 cloves*
2 tablespoons double	*4 peppercorns*
cream	*1oz (25g) butter*
4oz (100g) white	*1 bayleaf*
bread crumbs	*Pinch of nutmeg*

Stick the cloves into the onion and place it into a pan with the milk, butter, peppercorns and bayleaf. Bring to just under boiling point and keep it hot for ¹/₂ hour. Remove from the heat, cover and let it stand a further ¹/₂ hour to infuse. Strain the milk into a clean pan and stir in the bread crumbs. Heat gently to just under simmering, for 30 minutes, stirring frequently. Season to taste, and stir in the cream and nutmeg.

GAME CHIPS

These are simply wafer thin rounds of potatoes deep fried to a golden brown. Packets of plain crisps may be substituted. Warm them in the cooling oven with the pheasant.

FRIED BREAD CRUMBS

To serve six people allow 4oz (100g) fresh white bread crumbs. Fry them in 2oz (50g) butter, or the reserved roasting fats until they are golden brown.

Other trimmings include a good gravy made with game stock and game jellies, such as Rowan or Redcurrant.

OT ROAST GUINEA FOWL

1 oven-ready guinea fowl	*¹/₄ pint (150ml) chicken stock*	*2oz (50g) butter*
1 onion finely sliced	*Salt and freshly ground*	*2 large tomatoes*
2 sticks celery, sliced	*black pepper*	*¹/₂ teaspoon thyme*
2oz (50g) smoked bacon,	*4oz (100g) button*	*glass dry sherry*
chopped	*mushrooms*	*1 bayleaf*
	2 cloves of garlic	*1 teaspoon paprika*

In 1oz (25g) of butter, sauté the bacon and then add the onion and celery. Cook until softened and transfer to the bottom of a slow cooker or deep casserole dish. Skin and chop the tomatoes and add to the pot. In the remaining butter, brown the guinea fowl. Place it breast down into the vegetables and sprinkle with the herbs and the seasonings. Add the stock and the sherry and cover the dish. Cook as follows:

In a slow cooker, cook for 7-10 hours on low. In the oven, cook for 2 -2¹/₂ hours at 325°F/ 170°C/Gas mark 3. Half way through the cooking, turn the guinea fowl breast up and add the button mushrooms.

To serve, place the guniea fowl on a serving dish and surround it with the whole mushrooms which can be removed with a slotted spoon. Remove the bayleaf and liquidise the vegetables and stock to make a sauce which can be reheated in a pan. ***Serves 4.***

 $\mathcal{S}$TOVED CHICKEN

In bygone days chicken was very much a festive dish. This simple way of cooking it recalls the age old, one-pot cooking method. Choose a free range chicken for better flavour, or use a guniea fowl.

8 small chicken joints	*1 pint (600ml) chicken stock*
2lb (900g) potatoes, peeled	*2oz (50g) butter*
and sliced	*2 onions sliced*
Salt& pepper	*Chopped parsley*

Grease a deep casserole dish, or if using a slow cooker switch it to "High". Brown the chicken joints in the butter. Place a layer of potato slices in the bottom of the casserole dish and then a layer of sliced onions. Season well with salt and pepper. Place 4 chicken joints over the vegetables and then repeat the layers ending with a layer of potatoes. Add the stock and cover with foil before putting on the lid. Cook as follows:

In a slow cooker, cook for 4-8 hours on low.In an oven, cook for 3 hours at 300°F/ 150°C/ Gas mark 2.

Serve garnished with chopped parsley.   **Serves 4**

VARIATION: *follow the recipe above but use a jointed rabbit and serve with a game jelly.*

42
~

HEN IN THE HEATHER

1 chicken, jointed
3floz (90ml) light cooking oil
4 floz (150g) clear heather honey
Salt and freshly ground black pepper
3oz (75g) French mustard
$\frac{1}{2}$ teaspoon curry powder
1 clove minced garlic

Put the chicken into an oven proof casserole. Combine all the other ingredients and pour over the chicken. Cover the dish and cook in the oven for one hour at 375°F/ 190°C/ Gas mark 4. Baste the chicken thoroughly and return to the oven for a further half hour without the lid so the chicken browns nicely.

Serves 4.

This recipe is an adaptation of one passed to me by an acquaintance years ago. It was a great favourite, both with guests at my hotel and also with my family. Few people can pick the secret ingredient which is the curry powder! Serve with fluffy creamed potatoes and lots of fresh vegetables.

Using heather honey is a luxury of course but you may economise with any convenient clear honey.

 TALKER'S PIE

Here's a simple variation of Shepherds's Pie. Venison is available minced from Game Butchers, or, you could use a food processor to mince a quantity of shoulder venison.

1lb (450g) minced venison
2 tablespoons olive oil or butter
1 tablespoon tomato paste
2 tablespoons Mushroom ketchup
¹/₂ pint (275ml) beef or game stock
Glass of port (optional)
1 large onion, chopped

Salt & pepper
Pinch of mixed herbs
Gravy granules
1lb (450g) hot mashed potato
Extra butter and grated cheese
for topping if liked.

In a heavy saucepan, sweat the onions in the oil over a low heat until soft. Add the venison and brown gently, stirring to prevent meat forming lumps. Add the seasoning, herbs, tomato paste and ketchup along with the stock and bring to simmering point. Cover and simmer gently for 20 minutes. If used, add the port and stir thoroughly.

Thicken the mixture with gravy granules and place into a pie dish. Top with hot mashed potato, a little butter and grated cheese and brown under a hot grill.

VARIATION: *top with a mixture of mashed turnip and potato* (clapshot)   **Serves 4**

VENISON AND RASPBERRIES

8 venison chops
2oz (50g) butter
Tablespoon olive oil
1 clove garlic, crushed

Sauce: 4oz (100g) raspberries
$\frac{1}{4}$ pint (150ml) stock
Glass of port
Pinch of sugar
Rowan jelly

Into a saucepan put half the raspberries, the stock, sugar and port. Cook very rapidly for several minutes so that the raspberries become soft as the sauce reduces. Strain the sauce and discard the pips.

In a heavy pan, melt the butter and oil and when hot add the garlic. Cook briefly and add the venison chops. They will only need a few minutes cooking each side and should be removed to a warm oven and covered while still pink.

Pour the sauce into the pan, combining with any juices and bring to the boil. Stir in a tablespoon of rowan jelly. Add half the remaining raspberries and simmer just enough to warm them

Serve the chops with the sauce and a few of the remaining fresh raspberries to garnish. **Serves 4.**

You can make quantities of this sauce to freeze and it can easily be served without the addition of the fresh raspberries.

LAMB AND BEEF

For most people in the 18th and 19th centuries, beef and lamb
remained luxury foods. Farmers sold their livestock for much needed cash and,
like the fisher folk, learned to make do with the poorer cuts for themselves.
Recipes making use of sheep's heads are now largely a curiosity.

Although agricultural improvements meant that livestock could
be kept alive through the harsh Scottish winters, food preservation in the home
was still a problem. Salting and pickling helped preserve meats and the use of
spices covered the taste of that which had become tainted.

For the many living in cramped city tenements, food preparation
was impossible. Baked meat pies were sold on the crowded city streets and
were a staple for those without cooking facilities.

As with Game, meats were mostly cooked in pots over the fire:
the best way to tenderise poorer cuts and keep the home warm at the same time.
Roasting was probably confined to the homes of the great and wealthy.

Since few traditional recipes have been passed on for beef
and lamb, the following collection represents a more modern approach
to the excellent produce and wonderful cooking facilities from
which most of us benefit today.

 ROSEN HOT POT

This traditional dish is cooked slowly, maximising the subtle flavours of the ingredients. The meat of this "poorer" cut of lamb practically melts with slow cooking making a hearty and economical dish.

$1^1/_2$ lb (675g) neck lamb, trimmed weight without fat	2 onions
1 can chopped tomatoes	2-3 carrots sliced
$^1/_2$ pint (300ml) white stock	Salt & pepper

Slice the meat or cut into large dice. Place layers of lamb, carrots and onions into an oven-proof casserole or slow-cooker and season each layer. Pour over the chopped tomatoes and juice. Add the stock. Cover tightly and cook as follows:

In an oven: for $2^1/_2$ - 3 hours at 325°F/ 160°C/ Gas mark 3.

In a slow cooker: on Low for 8-10 hours.

When cooked you may like to thicken the gravy slightly with granules or with cornflour and water in the usual way.

Serve with boiled new potatoes or mashed potatoes.   ***Serves 4***

UNDEE LAMB CHOPS

4 chump chops (cut from the leg)
2¹/₂ floz (75ml) vinegar
¹/₂ teaspoon ground ginger
4 tablespoons Dundee Marmalade
4 slices of orange to garnish
2oz (50g) butter
2¹/₂ floz (75ml) water
¹/₂ teaspoon paprika
Salt & pepper

Use a heavy based fry pan with a close fitting lid. Brown the chops in the butter. Sprinkle over the spices, salt and pepper, and add the water and vinegar. Place a tablespoon of marmalade on each chop. Bring to a slow simmer, cover and cook for about 45 minutes on a very low heat. Check the meat is tender. If required use just a little extra water.

The marmalade melts down to make a lovely tangy sauce. Garnish each chop with a twist of orange and serve with fresh vegetables and boiled potatoes.

Serves 4

CROFTER'S PIE

12oz (350g) minced lamb
4oz (100g) turnip, peeled and finely diced
4oz (100g) chopped onions
14oz (400g) tin chopped tomatoes
12oz (350g) shortcrust pastry
1 lamb or beef stock cube

Oil for cooking
Pinch mixed herbs
Salt & pepper
1¹/₂

Preheat the oven to 400°F/ 200°C/ Gas mark 6

Gently stir fry the meat, onions, garlic and turnip for 5 minutes so that the vegetables soften and the meat browns. Drain off any excess oil and stir in the flour, the crumbled stock cube and the herbs. Add the chopped tomatoes and juice and bring to simmering point, stirring constantly. Season according to taste and simmer for a further 5 minutes.

Grease an 8" (200mm) pie dish and line it with half of the rolled pastry. Fill with the cooked mixture and cover the pie with the remaining pastry. Seal the edges by pressing with a fork and pierce the top to make a vent. Brush with milk or beaten egg and bake for 30-35 minutes.

AGGIS

To prepare a haggis in the home requires time and strong desire for authenticity. Few people today really want to clean and prepare sheep's lungs and stomach bags. Top butchers sell fine haggis which can easily be boiled or quickly prepared in a micro-wave. Of course, it only approximates the real beast.

$\mathscr{P}$OT HAGGIS

8oz (225g) lamb heart
$^1/_2$lb (225g) minced lamb
8oz (225g) shredded suet
4oz (100g) pinhead oatmeal
4oz (100g) medium oatmeal

8oz (225g) lamb's liver
2 teaspoons salt
3 teaspoons pepper
$^1/_4$ teaspoon cayenne
$^1/_2$ teaspoon nutmeg

Mince the heart and the liver and combine with the minced lamb. Boil for half an hour and drain. Add all the other ingredients and mix thoroughly. Put it into one (or two) bowls and press down lightly. Cover with foil and tie tightly. Steam for $2^1/_2$ - 3 hours. To bake in an oven, add $^1/_4$ pint (150ml) stock to the mixture, cover and cook for $1^1/_2$ hours at 375°F/ 190°C/ Gas mark 5. When cooked, break it up with a fork and serve with neeps and tatties and a good gravy.

Serves 4-6 generously

SCOTCH PIES

Hot water pastry:	Filling:
1lb (450g) plain flour	1lb (450g) lean lamb, minced
6oz (175g) lard	Pinch of mace or nutmeg
6floz (225ml) water, approx.	Salt & pepper
Pinch of salt	$^1/_4$ pint (150ml) gravy
Milk for glazing	

Make the filling by combining the meat, spice and seasoning. Make the pastry by sifting the flour and salt into a warm bowl. Make a well in the centre. Melt the lard in a scant measure of the water and when bubbling add to the dry ingredients mixing thoroughly. Form into a ball and keep warm while using small amounts to make each pastry case. Do this by rolling a suitable amount for each pie and shaping the crust round the base of a glass (or jar) ensuring there are no cracks in the pastry. As the pastry firms and cools remove the glass and continue until you have about $^1/_4$ of the pastry left to make the lids.

Fill the cases with meat and add just the gravy.

Roll the remaining pastry and use the glass to cut the lids. Wet the edges and place over the pies pressing them down over the filling. Pinch the edges and trim, and make a small vent for the steam. Glaze with the milk and bake for about 45 minutes at 275°F/ 140°C/ Gas mark 1

Makes about 8-10.

ABERDEEN ANGUS STEAKS

For special occasions the best cuts of beef would have been roasted and enjoyed as a luxury. Here is a dish named to celebrate the famous Scottish Aberdeen Angus, the cattle bred in the early 19th century in the lushness of the Northern Lowlands.

4 pieces of topside or rump
*   *steak, 6-8oz (176g-225g) each*
1 teaspoon ground ginger
7oz (200g) chopped tomatoes
1 tablespoon Worcestershire
*   *sauce*
1¹/₂ tablespoons wine vinegar

1oz (25g) flour
oil for frying
2 cloves garlic, crushed
1oz (25g) brown sugar
1 tablespoon brown sauce
Salt & pepper
Parsley for garnish

Dust the steaks with a mixture of the flour and ground ginger and brown them quickly in hot oil. Place them in a shallow oven proof dish.

Mix all of the other ingredients to make the sauce and pour over the steaks. Cover the dish with a lid or with foil and cook for $1^1/_2$ hours in the oven at 325°F/ 170°C/ Gas mark 3.

Serve with roast potatoes and lightly cooked fresh vegetables.   **Serves 4.**

BEEF OLIVES

This his recipe is a "made-up" dish and appears in cookery books from about the turn of the century. It is a clever way to make a meal from a small amount of beef. Traditionally the stuffing contained suet which I have omitted.

8 thin rounds of topside, about	*4 tablespoons minced onion*
6" (15cm) diameter	*1 tablespoon chopped parsley*
Oil for frying	*1 egg beaten*
³/₄ pint (450ml) beef stock	*Salt & pepper*
Seasoned flour	*grated rind of a lemon*
Stuffing:	*1 teaspoon dried thyme*
4oz (100g) bread crumbs	*Milk to mix*

Combine all the forcemeat ingredients and form 8 sausage shapes. Place each on a beef round and wrap firmly. You may like to secure with a cocktail stick. Roll them in seasoned flour and brown them quickly in hot oil.

Place the olives in a shallow oven-proof dish and pour over the stock. Cover and cook in the oven for 1¹/₂hrs at 350°F/ 180°C/ Gas mark 4.

When cooked, remove the cocktail sticks, if used, and serve with mashed potatoes and vegetables. ***Serves 4***

$\mathcal{H}$ASTY BEEF OLIVES

$\mathbf{M}$any butchers make up beef olives, generally stuffed with some sort of sausage meat. This is a great time -saver though you will probably find it necessary to skim off the extra fat at the end of cooking.

Following, are some variations and ideas for using Beef Olives;

SEASONED SAUSAGE STUFFING

To 8-12oz (225-350g) pork or beef sausage meat add 2 teaspoons of chopped parsley and $^1/_2$ teaspoon dried herbs. Add a tablespoon of pinched oatmeal or bread crumbs and bind with a beaten egg.

VARIATIONS FOR THE STOCK SAUCE

Substitute part of the stock with red wine.
Add tomato puree or mushroom ketchup to the stock.
Use herbs, if liked.
Use a can or jar of prepared cooking sauce for a really
quick meal. Add sliced onions and carrots to the stock,
adding flavour and body to the dish.

HIGHLAND BEEF BALLS

The original recipe was devised as a method of preserving the meat for up to ten days and required suet in large quantities as well as spices and saltpetre. The uncooked, richly larded balls were then covered in more suet before storing!

1lb (450g) minced beef
¹/₂ teaspoon ginger
1 teaspoon ground black pepper
¹/₂ teaspoon brown sugar
¹/₂ teaspoon mace or cumin

1 egg, beaten
¹/₂ teaspoon allspice
1 teaspoon salt
¹/₂ teaspoon ground cloves
Oil for deep frying

Mix the spices, seasoning and sugar together and then mix thoroughly into the minced beef. Bind the mixture with the egg. Form into equal-sized balls and deep fry to a golden brown. Serve with Rumbledthumps or Colcannon and a beef gravy.

Serves 4.

OUGH IN THE POT

Traditions in brewing ales and beers are ancient and complex. In the 13th century, in the Borders for example, the peasants grew oats and bere (a grain crop). The oats were eaten and the bere was taken to the village brewster who generally rented a brew-house from the local abbey! Ale was the only alternative to water for drinking purposes. It is easy to imagine how it ended up in the cooking pot!

1¹/₂ lb (675g) hough, or shin beef	*2 onions sliced*
¹/₂ pint (300ml) stout or dark ale	*1 tablespoon oil*
3 tablespoons soy sauce	*Seasoned flour*
1 tablespoon mushroom ketchup	*Black pepper*

Slice the meat into steaks and dust with the seasoned flour. Brown the meat in hot oil and place in an oven proof casserole or slow cooker with the sliced onions. Bring the stout and sauces to the boil and pour over the meat and onions. Cover and cook as follows: in an oven for 3-4 hours at 325°F/ 170°C/ Gas mark 3; in a slow-cooker for 6-8 hours on "low"

Thicken the gravy before serving if necessary. Mashed potatoes and a choice of root and green vegetables go well with this very hearty dish. ***Serves 4.***

ℳUSSELBURGH PIE

Musselburgh, just outside Edinburgh was once the city's source for oysters and mussels. There are still Oyster bars in Edinburgh recalling the days when oyster parties were held in the taverns of old town.

$1^1/_2$lb (675g) rump steak, cut very thinly and into strips

$1^1/_2$oz (35g) beef suet

2 tablespoons oil

8oz (225g) prepared puff pastry

3lb (1.5kg) fresh mussels

2 onions, finely chopped

$^1/_2$ pint (300ml) water

Seasoned flour

Salt & pepper

Cook the mussels in about 2" (5cm) boiling water for 2-3 minutes with the lid on the pan. Remove the mussels from their shells.

Lay 2-3 mussels and a small piece of suet on each strip of steak and roll tightly. Dip them in seasoned flour and place around a pie funnel in a 2 pint (1L) pie dish.

Cook the onions in the oil until softened and add them to the pie. Season and add the water and cover the dish with foil. Cook for $1^1/_2$ hours in the oven set at 350°F/ 180°C/ Gas mark 3. Let this cool before adding the pastry lid which may be decorated and glazed with a little milk. Make several ventilation holes and then bake for 30 minutes in a hot oven at 425°F/ 220°C/ Gas mark 7. ***Serves 4-6.***

YRSHIRE MEAT LOAF

 T his is an adaptation of a dish which used to be boiled in a cloth in much the same way as Cloutie dumpling. Preparing it as a meat loaf is less involved and appropriate for today's busy lifestyle.

1lb (450g) Ayrshire bacon, minced*	*2 eggs, beaten*
1lb (450g) minced beef	*1 onion, minced*
$^{1}/_{4}$ teaspoon ground nutmeg	*3oz (75g) oatmeal*
3oz (75g) fresh bread crumbs	*Salt & pepper*
Stock to moisten	

Combine all the ingredients thoroughly, using only enough stock to assist in binding the mixture. Place it in a loaf tin, cover with foil and bake for $1^{1}/_{2}$ hours in the oven set at 350°F/ 180°C/ Gas mark 4. This may be eaten hot or cold.

Serves 6-8 generously.

* Ayrshire bacon is sliced from the rolled side of pork and contains both lean and fat bacon. If using a substitute, ensure that half the quantity is streaky bacon.

Tɪᴘ: line the tin with foil to make it easy to remove. Serve on a plate. It looks most impressive.

Vᴀʀɪᴀᴛɪᴏɴs: *Substitute sausage meat for all or part of the bacon.Chopped herbs may be used, if liked.*

SEA PIE

It is generally thought this recipe from the North East made a warming meal of scraps of beef for the coastal fishermen. It has a traditional suet pastry and is cooked on the stove top.

$1^1/_2$lb (675g) stewing beef, diced
6oz (175g) carrot, diced
6oz (175g) turnip, diced
1 medium onion, finely chopped
Cold water
1 tablespoon plain flour
Salt & pepper

Oil for frying
For the pastry:
8oz (250g) self-raising flour
4oz (100g) shredded suet
$^1/_4$ pint (150ml) water
Salt & pepper

In a pan or flameproof casserole, soften the onion in the oil and add the beef, cooking until browned. Add the vegetables and season with salt and pepper. Stir thoroughly and add just enough water to cover the mixture. Cover with a lid and simmer gently for an hour.

Make the pastry by sifting the flour into a bowl, adding the shredded suet and seasoning well. Add only sufficient water to make a fairly stiff but elastic dough. Roll it to fit easily into the pan or casserole.

Sprinkle the flour over the stew and stir. Add the pastry topping. Cover the lid and cook for another 30 minutes.

Serves 4.

ORFAR BRIDIES

1¹/₂lb (675g) rump steak
2 onions, finely chopped
3oz (75g) shredded suet or butter
Milk for glazing

1¹/₂lb (675g) prepared shortcrust
or puff pastry
Salt & pepper

Beat the steak with a meat hammer or rolling pin and cut into thin strips. Beat the steak again and cut to pieces no longer than 1" (125mm). Season well and add the onion and the suet, mixing thoroughly.

Divide the pastry into four and roll each to an oval shape. Pile the meat mixture along the centre of each pastry oval and dampen the edges of the pastry. Bring up the sides of the pastry to form a seam down the centre by pinching firmly together. Make a vent to allow steam to escape and brush with a little milk. Bake in a hot oven for 20 minutes at 400°F/ 200°C/ Gas mark 6, and then lower the temperature to 350°F/ 180°C/ Gas mark 4 and bake the bridies for a further 45 minutes. *Serves 4.*

VARIATIONS: Substitute top quality lean minced beef for the steak to make a quick family meal.

The onions may be omitted. In the old days a Bridie had two holes to indicate the inclusion of onions!

SAVOURIES, SNACKS AND VEGETABLES

The following recipes are a peculiar reflection on traditions
in Scottish cooking. Most of them are very simple and therefore ideally
suited to our busy pace of life. They also reflect the Scottish sense of
humour. Try to keep a straight face when you serve
Clapshot or Rumbledethumps!

I include the recipe for "Fitless Cock" because it is so odd
and also, like Skirlie, it evolved from the need to use what resources were
close at hand. Oats were the staple before the coming of the potato. My butcher
was amused by this recipe and took a slice home to try with his supper!
I devised a microwave version which better suits today's lifestyle.
It is surprisingly good.

Until the 19th century the use of vegetables was restricted,
kail being the prime green leaf used. The following saying sums
up the thrifty Scots attitude.

"Kail hains bread
Kail saves bread"

Once the potato became commonplace, Scottish ingenuity
soon turned this versatile vegetable into a staple, devising
some very original recipes with equally original names!

SCOTCH EGGS

8 hard boiled eggs
1½ lb (675g) pork sausage meat
Pinch of mace
4oz (100g) crisp bread crumbs

1 egg, beaten
Seasoned flour
Salt & pepper
Oil for deep frying

Boil the eggs for ten minutes, stirring occasionally to keep the yolk in the centre. Cool quickly under cold running water and shell the eggs, allowing them to get quite cold.

Season the sausage meat adding the mace. Roll the eggs in the seasoned flour and then cover each egg with the sausage meat making it about ¼" (5mm) thick, ensuring it is firmly packed.

Dip the eggs into the beaten egg and roll each in the bread crumbs. Deep fry until browned evenly.

Scotch eggs may be eaten hot though they are commonly served cold. They are an ideal snack or make a good addition to a salad.   ***Serves 4-8.***

$\mathscr{S}$KIRLIE

This is a dish named after the sizzling sound of the cooking! It should be made with best quality dripping or suet and can be served with game or roast meats. Try it as a stuffing for chicken or turkey- in which case, add a glass of whisky too! Originally, this easy dish from Aberdeenshire was served as a meal with mashed potatoes, called chappit tatties.

> *2oz (50g) dripping or suet*
> *6oz (175g) medium oatmeal (approx.)*
> *Salt & pepper*
> *2 medium onions, finely chopped*

Melt the fat and when quite hot add the onions, browning them well. Add enough of the oatmeal to absorb the fat, stirring constantly. Season well and cook for several minutes longer. The mixture should be quite thick.

Serves 4 as a accompaniment

$\mathscr{S}$TOVIES

As with the recipe for Stoved Chicken, this simple cottage recipe was cooked in the iron pot over the hearth. It is still widely popular as a filling snack, often sold in baker's shops or sandwich bars for lunches.

2lb (900g) evenly sized potatoes,
peeled and sliced thickly
2oz (50g) meat dripping or butter

Salt & pepper
2 onions, peeled thinly
¹/₂ pint (300ml) water

In a heavy saucepan, melt the dripping or butter and cook the onions gently for several minutes until they begin to soften. Add the potatoes and stir through the butter and onions. Add the water, bring to the boil and then simmer very gently in the pan, covered with a tight fitting lid. Stir occasionally to prevent sticking. The potatoes should remain in large chunks.Serves 4-6

VARIATIONS: *Replace the water with stock and during the last ten minutes of cooking, add 8oz (225g) cooked diced meat.*

A QUICK VARIATION FROM THE BORDERS
Boil the potatoes with the onion in salted water until just cooked. Drain and allow the potatoes to dry out over a low heat for a few minutes before adding the dripping and any meat. Reheat, stirring, allowing the potatoes to break up a little.

 FITLESS COCK

When Meg Dods included this in her collection of traditional Scottish dishes in 1826 it was considered an ancient dish. Like other oatmeal dishes or puddings, it is suitable as an accompaniment to game or fowl though it was traditionally served as a meal itself on Fastern's Eve, the night before Lent. Thus it was called a "fastyn " or "festy" cock

4oz (100g) medium oatmeal
1 medium onion, finely chopped
Salt & pepper

2oz (50g) shredded suet
1 large egg, beaten

Mix the oats, suet and onion thoroughly and season well. Bind the mixture with the beaten egg, adding a little water if necessary so that you have a firm ball. Shape it like a dressed chicken. Cook in a covered dish suitable for the microwave, on Mark 8 for 5-6 minutes. It should feel dry on the outside and firm to the touch. Do not overcook.

Lay it on a serving dish, as you would for a roast chicken, so it can be cut at the table. Serves 4-6 as an accompaniment.

VARIATION: *Use as a substantial stuffing for chicken - in which case, add a glass of whisky!*

SCOTS POTATO FRITTERS

(adapted from a recipe of
Lady Harriet St. Clair)
*4 large potatoes, scrubbed or
   peeled*
1 tablespoon fine bread crumbs
Olive oil for cooking
Salt & pepper
1 large egg, beaten
1 tablespoon minced cooked ham

Boil the potatoes until just under cooked. Slice them thickly. Make a mixture of the egg, breadcrumbs and ham and season lightly. Heat the oil and after dipping the potatoes in the egg mixture, fry them in small batches.

Serve with steaks and other fried or grilled meats.   ***Serves 4.***

QUICK POTATO SCONES

8oz (225g) mashed potato
*$^{1}/_{2}$oz (10g) butter,
   approximately*
Oil for cooking
2oz (50g) plain flour
$^{1}/_{4}$ teaspoon salt

Combine all the ingredients thoroughly and pat into thin rounds or roll and cut into traditional triangles. Cook in a heavy pan, over a high heat with a minimum amount of oil for about three minutes each side.

They are generally served these days at breakfast.

RUMBLEDTHUMPS

Here's a splendidly named dish from the Borders, one which certainly intrigues those who have never come across it before. The name derives from the sound of the beating spoon against the pan and I imagine some canny mother of the past came up with the name to entice a reluctant child to eat this simple homely dish.

> *1lb (450g) potatoes, mashed with butter, salt and pepper*
> *1oz (25g) butter*
> *1lb (450g) shredded cooked cabbage*
> *Salt & pepper*

Combine the hot potato with the hot cabbage adding the butter. Season to taste. ***Serves 4.***

VARIATIONS: *Add chopped chives or an onion chopped and cooked. Put the combined mixture into an oven proof dish, top with grated cheese and brown in the oven.*

Use up leftovers by making flat round cakes and frying in hot oil for breakfast.

Kailkenny: using the basic recipe, add two table-spoons of double cream to replace the butter.

OLCANNON

1lb (459g) potatoes, mashed with butter,
  salt and pepper
8oz (225g) diced carrot
8oz (225g) diced turnip
1 tablespoon good brown sauce
1lb (450g) shredded cooked cabbage
2oz 950g) butter
Salt & pepper

Cook the carrot and turnip together until soft enough to mash into a smooth purée. In a large pan, melt the butter and add the cabbage, potato and the purée, stirring thoroughly to combine and heat through evenly. Add the brown sauce and season to taste.

Serves 4-6

Colcannon is a Highland dish with Irish origins while Clapshot is a dish from Orkney.

LAPSHOT

1lb (450g) potatoes,
  mashed
2oz (50g) butter
Chopped chives
1lb (450g) turnip
  mashed
Salt & pepper

Combine the hot mashed potato and turnip, season and stir in the chives. Melt the butter in a large pan and reheat the mixture gently to a very high heat.

Serves 4-6.

SCOTS POTATO PIE

4 large potatoes of even sizes
12oz (350g) minced meat
Ketchup of choice
oil for cooking

1 onion, finely chopped
Salt & pepper
³/₄ pint (450ml) gravy

Peel the potatoes finely and shape each one just enough to let it lie flat. Cut the tops, about ¹/₂" (1cm) thick and reserve. Carefully hollow the potatoes so that you have a shell about ¹/₂" (1cm) thick. (I use an apple corer)

Brown the mince with the onion, adding ketchup and seasoning to taste. Moisten with a little gravy. Put the mixture into the potatoes but do not over fill and cap them with the potato lids which can be secured with cocktail sticks. Preheat oil in a roasting tin, add the potatoes and baste with hot oil. Roast in the oven for approximately one hour at 425°F/ 220°C/ Gas mark 7. Baste with more oil from time to time. The length of cooking time will depend upon the size of the potatoes. Serve with the gravy. *Serves 4.*

There are several regional variations using this basic idea. Perhaps the most unusual, Shetland Liver Koogs, calls for a stuffing of fish livers. The potatoes were cooked in the peat fires and one imagines a fisherman's family round the hearth!

$\mathscr{B}$ANFFSHIRE POTATO PIES

4 large potatoes of
  even sizes
1egg yolk
3floz (30ml) milk, approx.
3oz fresh bread crumbs
1oz (25g) butter
Pinch dried mixed herbs
Salt & pepper

Prepare the potatoes as for
the Scots potato pies. Cream
the butter, add the egg yolk and
beat thoroughly. Add the herbs
and the bread crumbs and
combine well using sufficient
milk to bind. Season to taste
and stuff the
potatoes.
Cook as for
the Scots
potato pies.

$\mathscr{A}$NGUS POTATO PIES

4 large baking potatoes
8oz (225g) Finnan-haddie or,
  other smoked fish, cooked
2oz (50g) butter
Milk to mix
Salt& pepper

Bake the potatoes until soft and cut
a small round from the tops. Scoop out all
the potato and mash $^3/_4$ of it with the
butter. Flake the fish and combine with the
mashed potato using a little milk to
moisten. Season and fill the potato shells,
piling the mixture high. Top with the lids
and heat through in the oven.

NOTE: *in all of the above recipes I
have used 8-12oz (225-350g) potatoes
which is sufficient for a serving as a lunch
or for supper.*

70
~

PAN HAGGERTY

1lb (450g) potatoes
2oz (50g) dripping
Salt & pepper
$^1/_2$lb (225g) sliced onions
5oz (150g) grated cheese

Peel the potatoes and slice quite finely. Heat the dripping in a heavy lidded fry pan and put in the potatoes and onions in layers, seasoning each layer lightly and adding a sprinkle of cheese. Reserve 1oz (25g) of the cheese for the topping.

Cover and cook over a gentle heat for about 45 minutes, or until the potatoes are cooked. Remove the lid, sprinkle over the remaining cheese and brown under a hot grill.

Serves 4.

STOVIE'n OAT CAKES

1lb (450g) mashed potatoes
1 egg beaten
1oz (25g) butter
Salt & pepper
Leftover cold meat, minced
1 onion, minced
Medium oatmeal

Combine the potato, meat, onion and butter and season to taste. Bind with just a little of the egg and form into cakes. Coat with the beaten egg and sprinkle over the oatmeal, turning the cakes and repeating the coating. Fry in hot oil.   **Serves 4.**

Of course, you could use up leftover stovies this way!

A SCOTS RABBIT

adapted from Meg Dods's recipe

4oz (100g) grated cheddar	$^1/_4$ *pint (150ml) brown ale*
2 teaspoons mustard powder	*2 tablespoons flour*
Freshly ground black pepper	*Salt*
4 slices buttered toast	*Knob of butter*

Put the grated cheese into a saucepan and stir in the mustard powder and the flour with a pinch of salt and some pepper. Stir in the ale and then place over a low to medium heat. Bring to simmering point, stirring all the time and adding the knob of butter. When the mixture is thick and bubbly pour over the toast.

Serves 4.

This used to be made in a "cheese toaster", a dish which has a compartment which is filled with hot water, allowing the cheese to be served at the table and kept warm. Toast was then dipped into the cheese. A Scottish fondue!

VARIATIONS : *Use Stilton and substitute the ale with milk or a dry white wine. Prepared mustard may be used instead of the powder.*

COTS TOASTS

I suppose most of us wonder how simple bread and butter came to be a feature of afternoon teas in days gone by! Toasted bread is primarily associated with breakfast these days and is sadly overlooked as the basis of a quick snack - or maybe it is too humble to be included in most collections of recipes! I think it is an ideal way of sharing a treat or presenting a "wee" taste of Scotland for unexpected visitors

Here are some simple ideas.

SALMON TOAST

Allow 4oz (100g) cold cooked flaked salmon per slice of toast. Bind the salmon with the smallest possible amount of Hollandaise sauce, season lightly and pile it on to thick slices of toast. Garnish with wafer-thin slices of cucumber and a wedge of lemon.

SMOKEY TOASTS

For each slice of toast allow 4oz (100g) flaked and cooked smoked fish. Heat it gently in a little butter, add a small amount of double cream to bind and serve immediately on buttered toast. Garnish with a little chopped parsley and a wedge of lemon.

73
~

GAME TOAST

Use up leftover game by mincing it and moistening it with some thick gravy. Season with a little salt and freshly ground black pepper. Serve on hot buttered toast with a game jelly.

VENISON TOAST

Since minced venison can be bought easily this is an ideal toast topper to make and freeze. It will then be on hand for unexpected visitors or that lazy Sunday evening! Use the basic recipe for Stalker's Pie (see page 44) serving suitable amounts on hot toast with a game jelly on the side.

HAGGIS TOAST

Allow about 4oz (100g) cooked haggis per slice of toast. heat it through with a good gravy and serve on toast. Tomato slices make a refreshing garnish.

GLASGOW HAM 'n' HADDIE TOAST

Allow a slice of smoked ham and 4oz (100g) cooked flaked smoked haddock per slice of toast. Heat the fish with a little butter and stir in a little double cream. Quickly heat the ham slices in a little butter and lay on the hot toast. Pile on the fish and serve immediately. Garnish with chopped chives.

SCOTS WOODCOCK

The original recipe calls for the use of egg yolks rather than whole eggs: a rather elegant and expensive form of scrambled eggs.

4 eggs	*4 rounds toast*
Anchovy paste	*Single cream*
1oz (50g) butter	*Pinch cayenne*
Salt & pepper	*Chopped parsley*

In a small saucepan, melt the butter. Beat the eggs with 4 tablespoons of cream in a jug and season lightly. Pour into the melting butter. Cook the eggs, stirring all the while.

Spread anchovy paste onto the toast and pile on the eggs. Add the tiniest sprinkle of cayenne and a little chopped parsley.

VARIATION: *Instead of using Anchovy paste, put the eggs onto buttered toast and lay an anchovy fillet across the top.*

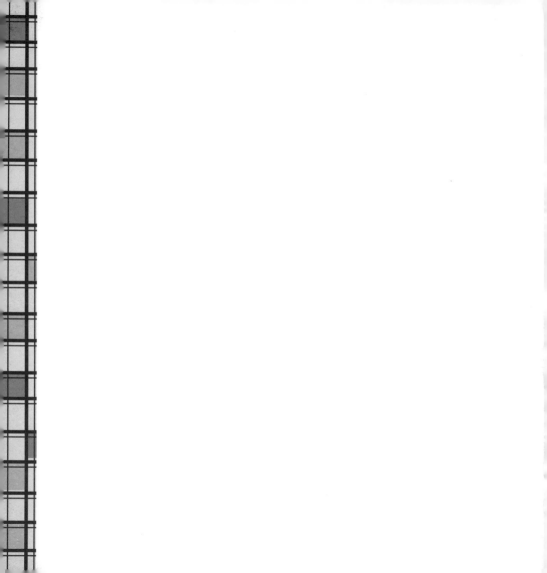

NOTES FOR AMERICAN COOKS

In Britain, weighing with scales is the usual way to measure ingredients, whereas in America the 8fl oz cup is used.

Following is a general guide to the most common ingredients, their American equivalents and their weight conversions.

The British Pint is 20 Fluid oz. while the American Pint is 16 fluid oz. Use $2^1/_2$ cups.

Compared to the British tablespoon which measures 17.7 ml the American tablespoon holds 14.2 ml. Use a rounded measure.

The teaspoon measure is the same in both countries.

8oz Plain flour - All purpose flour - $2^1/_2$ *cups*

8oz Self-Raising flour- All purpose self-rising flour - $2^1/_3$ *cups*

8oz oatmeal, fine or medium - *2 cups*

8oz pinhead oatmeal, Irish oatmeal - $2^1/_4$ *cups*

8oz sugar- $1^1/_4$ *cups*

8oz butter, margarine - *1 cup*

8oz dripping- meat dripping - *1 cup*

8oz suet - *2 cups*

8oz minced beef- ground beef - *2 cups*

4oz fresh bread crumbs - *2 cups*

4oz grated cheese - *1 cup*

SOME COMMODITIES

Anchovy Essence or Sauce-	Anchovy Paste
Cornflour-	Cornstarch
Cream, double-	Whipping cream
single-	Light cream
Hough-	Shin or Shank of beef

Mushroom Ketchup is not always easy to get and Worcestershire Sauce may be substituted though it is quite a degree more spicy.

Instant mashed potato is a handy commodity for thickening soups and even stews.

Gravy Granules are a great boon in a busy kitchen and I believe our great grandmothers would have been delighted by this time saver.

Likewise, Thickening Granules are a great improvement on the cornflour- and -water method of thickening sauces.

Seasoned flour can be made up in quantity with plain flour, salt and pepper to taste and then stored.

INDEX

NOTES

NOTES

_____

_____

_____

_____

_____

_____

_____

_____

_____

_____

_____

_____

_____

_____

_____

NOTES